THE RUBY SUNRISE

SUNRISE

BY **RINNE GROFF**

★

DRAMATISTS
PLAY SERVICE
INC.

2

THE RUBY SUNRISE was commissioned by Playwrights Horizons with funds provided by the Harold and Mimi Steinberg Commissioning Program; developed with the assistance of the Sundance Theater Lab; and premiered by Trinity Rep and Actors Theatre of Louisville.

THE RUBY SUNRISE received its New York premiere at The Public Theater on November 1, 2005. It was directed by Oskar Eustis; the set design was by Eugene Lee; the costume design was by Deb Newhall; the lighting design was by Deb Sullivan; and the sound design was by Bray Poor. The cast was as follows:

SUZIE TYRONE .... Audra Blaser
HENRY, PAUL .... Benjamin Patch Darragh
TAD ROSE .... Jason Butler Harner
RUBY, ELIZABETH .... Marin Ireland
MARTIN MARCUS .... Richard Masur
LOIS, ETHEL REED .... Anne Scurria
LULU .... Maggie Siff

PART ONE

CHARACTERS

RUBY — young, maybe 17

HENRY — 21

LOIS — 40s–50s

PLACE

Boarding house in Indiana.

TIME

1927.

PART TWO

CHARACTERS

LULU — production girl, 20s

TAD ROSE — writer, late 20s–30s

MARTIN MARCUS — producer, 40s–50s

SUZIE TYRONE — actress, 20s

PAUL BENJAMIN — actor who played Henry in Part One

ETHEL REED — actress who played Lois

ELIZABETH HUNTER — actress who played Ruby

PLACE

New York City.

TIME

1952.

PART THREE

CHARACTERS, PLACE AND TIME

A combination of Parts One and Two

THE RUBY SUNRISE

PART ONE

Scene 1

A barn in Indiana, late on a January night in 1927. Ruby, a young woman, bundled up for warmth, becomes visible in the shadows. She has a rag in her hand. Various parts of a disassembled mechanical generator are strewn before her on the floor. She talks to the audience.

RUBY. It happened just like this. I was on the mower, doing a boy's job since my brothers had all fallen in the war or after to influenza. I was riding down the field, plowing the earth, each row, all those straight, straight lines. But my thoughts, as usual, weren't on farming; I was building something else in my mind. When the reins slipped out of my hands, I didn't even note it, which can be mighty dangerous, specially with a skittish horse like we had. And right then, right as the horse felt its freedom and jerked me forward with its pull …
HENRY. *(From offstage.)* Hey in there! *(Ruby stops still.)* Who's messing in there? *(Ruby sits. She begins rubbing kerosene into the generator parts.)* You best get out of there. You best move on. I got a gun. You coming out? 'Cause I'm coming in. You coming out? 'Cause I'm coming in. *(Henry enters with a lantern and a big piece of wood. Ruby continues cleaning the disassembled generator.)* What the devil…?
RUBY. Is 'cause of the storm.
HENRY. Huh?
RUBY. Snow storm out there.
HENRY. I know that. Who the heck are you?
RUBY. Miss Haver …
HENRY. You her's?

RUBY. Kind of.

HENRY. What kind?

RUBY. Aunt.

HENRY. You her niece?

RUBY. I been here before, when I was a kid.

HENRY. What are you doing here now?

RUBY. My daddy passed.

HENRY. Miss Haver didn't say about a funeral.

RUBY. Weren't close anymore.

HENRY. Doesn't your mamma need you now?

RUBY. My mamma died before I was rightly born. I'm alone.

HENRY. You got brothers? A sister?

RUBY. Just me now, okay? No one.

HENRY. So you're staying in the house?

RUBY. For a bit.

HENRY. I'm Henry. Henry Hudnut. I board here.

RUBY. Ruby. That your gun?

HENRY. No. Yeah. No. *(Henry sets down the piece of wood.)* Sorry about your daddy.

RUBY. Mnnnhmmm.

HENRY. I wouldn't've yelled like that if I'd known. Just it's black dark out there: Our power line is out, on account of the ice.

RUBY. That's what I'm taking care of.

HENRY. What you're taking care of?

RUBY. The Delco.

HENRY. A generator? That right there is a generator? I didn't even know Miss Haver had one.

RUBY. Mess of grease, isn't working.

HENRY. She'll be peeved you took it to shreds.

RUBY. I'm fixing it.

HENRY. Where'd you learn to do that?

RUBY. My daddy taught me.

HENRY. He's some kind of engineer? Was.

RUBY. Not with a degree kind.

HENRY. You know what you're doing?

RUBY. You partial to degrees?

HENRY. I'm getting one myself. At the School of Agriculture, Purdue. It's a good time for agro-business. And it's the best school in Indiana. I'll most like take over my daddy's feed store soon as I'm done — couple months away is all — not that I need a degree for that. You're making me nervous.

RUBY. Idle hands. Wanna help?

HENRY. Can't say I can. Don't get electricity perfectly. *(Ruby holds out a pair of wires to Henry.)*

RUBY. Take these wires here and link 'em up with your tongue.

HENRY. No, sir.

RUBY. Seems like you got it perfect enough.

HENRY. You were kidding with me? About putting it to my tongue?

RUBY. Ummm, yes, I was.

HENRY. *(Looking at the equipment.)* It sure doesn't look like much of anything now, huh?

RUBY. You think?

HENRY. Nothing like something to light up the whole house.

RUBY. That's 'cause of how I took it all apart.

HENRY. But all in parts, it's not a generator.

RUBY. Is so. Now more than ever, when you can see every inch of how it works.

HENRY. Maybe *you* can see how it works.

RUBY. Maybe I can. *(Ruby returns to her work, cleaning the grease of the equipment.)*

HENRY. Be careful with that oil. Farm the next county over had a fire started that way.

RUBY. What way?

HENRY. *(He doesn't know the details.)* Oil. Just there was a fire.

RUBY. I'll be careful. *(She continues with her work. Henry picks up a spare rag and, following Ruby's lead, begins to clean the equipment with her.)*

HENRY. I'll be careful, too.

Scene 2

The Kitchen. Later that morning. Lois, a woman in her early fifties, wearing a housecoat, holds a nearly full coffee pot.

LOIS. Who the hell made coffee? *(Henry enters.)*

HENRY. Morning, Miss Haver.

LOIS. Don't scream; I got a headache. You make coffee?

HENRY. Must've been Ruby.

9

LOIS. Ruby?

HENRY. I didn't know you had a generator.

LOIS. What are you talking about?

HENRY. She fixed your generator. Got the lights back on. *(Henry turns the switch on a light. It works. Henry and Lois look at the working light bulb.)*

LOIS. I'll be damned. *(Ruby enters. Lois turns to her.)* Ruby Sunrise.

RUBY. Morning.

LOIS. I'm looking at a ghost.

RUBY. Not likely.

LOIS. You got your mamma's hair, her eyes.

RUBY. I got my own eyes.

LOIS. When'd you get here?

HENRY. Imagine me: I found her in the barn.

LOIS. Henry, you're gonna be late for your class.

HENRY. It's not yet seven.

LOIS. You don't wanna be late.

HENRY. Morning, Miss Haver. Morning, Ruby.

RUBY. Morning. *(Henry leaves.)*

LOIS. What'd you do to that boy?

RUBY. Nothing.

LOIS. I don't want you messing with him. He's a good boy.

RUBY. Seems like.

LOIS. Where'd you sleep?

RUBY. You mean last night?

LOIS. It's bitter cold out there.

RUBY. It is.

LOIS. How'd you get here, Ruby?

RUBY. I need a place to stay.

LOIS. Excuse me?

RUBY. I would like to stay with you for a while.

LOIS. For how come?

RUBY. My daddy passed.

LOIS. Son of a bitch passed, huh?

RUBY. Mmmnhmmm.

LOIS. Isn't there folks back in Kokomo who need you?

RUBY. I'm the youngest.

LOIS. 'Course; I knew that. How old are you? You must be ... You pregnant?

RUBY. No.

LOIS. You don't look pregnant.

RUBY. I'm not pregnant.

LOIS. You can't stay here.

RUBY. I fixed your Delco. *(Lois turns the light off.)*

LOIS. Don't need a Delco.

RUBY. I could straighten out all your wires. Whole set-up is a mess, no wonder it shorts.

LOIS. You some angel sent to look in on my electrical?

RUBY. Didn't say angel.

LOIS. You sure you're not pregnant?

RUBY. I never even kissed somebody.

LOIS. Two weeks. Then you're on your way.

RUBY. Need three months.

LOIS. How come three months?

RUBY. You got a radio here?

LOIS. Who's asking who questions? Two weeks. Is fourteen days, up and over on a Thursday. I can't afford to feed you past then even if I wanted to.

RUBY. I'm gonna make it you got light in every room.

LOIS. I can't pay for that.

RUBY. Who said pay? Electrons running out there all along miles of wire. We'll just borrow them.

LOIS. Take whatever you want and to hell with the consequences. Sounds familiar.

RUBY. I'm not my mamma. Electrons ought to be free anyway. Like air, like water. I'll rig it for you.

LOIS. Did I ask you for light?

RUBY. Long as I'm here.

LOIS. Two weeks.

RUBY. Right; long as I'm here right now.

Scene 3

Night. The Kitchen. Lois sits at a table. She is drinking from an old red glass bottle. Henry enters.

HENRY. Hey, Miss Haver, have you seen my radio? It wasn't on my shelf; I thought maybe … Miss Haver, what are you doing with that bottle? That home brew?

LOIS. Hello, Henry.

HENRY. Better put it away. Could get you arrested.

LOIS. Johnny Law understands when a lady needs to pour herself a drink at certain junctures.

HENRY. Junctures?

LOIS. You judging me?

HENRY. No, Miss Haver. I just hate to see you blue.

LOIS. Who says I'm blue?

HENRY. When you're drinking.

LOIS. Maybe I'm celebrating. When's your birthday?

HENRY. Aww, Miss Haver.

LOIS. What, we can't celebrate your birthday?

HENRY. Today's not my birthday.

LOIS. We can celebrate it anyway. Here, have a drink.

HENRY. I couldn't.

LOIS. Easy. You could do it easy. To your twenties. *(Lois drinks. Henry doesn't.)*

HENRY. How old's Ruby?

LOIS. What?

HENRY. And why do you call her a sunrise?

LOIS. Will you kill that girl for me? Will you set a fire to the barn while she sleeps? If she ever sleeps. Lights on out there all the time.

HENRY. How she got electricity to the barn, I'll never know.

LOIS. Crafty. Like her mamma. And a lot of good it did *her.*

HENRY. I feel sorry for Ruby: she's alone in the world.

LOIS. That's the way they like it. Crafty dreamers. They're on a mission.

HENRY. What's Ruby's mission?

LOIS. Who cares; she's leaving in ten days.

HENRY. Mission isn't bad.

LOIS. If you don't care who you hurt to do it, it is. Better not to have hopes.

HENRY. Everybody's got hopes.

LOIS. Not me; no more; no, sir. I'm free. My aspiration crushed a long time ago.

HENRY. Let me take that bottle.

LOIS. I wrapped it up in the prettiest package when I was a girl. Bows and ribbons and fancy paper. And the man I thought was the most beautiful man in the world, he took those hopes and sent them away as a wedding gift to someone else.

HENRY. I know, Miss Haver.

LOIS. May you never have to feel what it feels: to want something more than anything in the world, and not only is it ripped from you but then it's exposed as poison, the kind that'll kill you.

HENRY. I know, Miss Haver.

LOIS. What do you know?

HENRY. I know what you told me before.

LOIS. I told you before?

HENRY. Couple times.

LOIS. I must be drunk.

HENRY. Are you going on up to bed now?

LOIS. Do you think I'm terrible?

HENRY. No, Miss Haver.

LOIS. Have you ever called me Lois?

HENRY. No, Miss Haver. *(Lois exits. Henry begins to clean up after her. Ruby enters. She has been loitering just outside the house, waiting for Lois's departure. Henry has the half-empty liquor bottle in his hand.)*

RUBY. You gonna drink that?

HENRY. Ruby.

RUBY. You want it?

HENRY. I was gonna dump it. There are laws.

RUBY. I need that alcohol.

HENRY. Maybe Miss Haver wants it.

RUBY. Be cursing the whole lot in the morning, how much she drank.

HENRY. But she wouldn't want *you* to take it.

RUBY. That's not saying much.

HENRY. What's she got against you?

RUBY. That I look like my mamma.

HENRY. What's she got against your mamma?

RUBY. You bribing me for gossip?

HENRY. Maybe.

RUBY. Aunt Lois used to love my daddy, and then he ran off with her sister. Gonna hand it over now?

HENRY. That was your daddy? Miss Haver talks about that man like the devil himself. *(Catching himself.)* May he rest in peace.

RUBY. Mmmnhmmm.

HENRY. Why'd you come here if that was your daddy?

RUBY. Where'd you want me to go?

HENRY. You got no place to go, huh?

RUBY. Look, I'll return your radio. I was just borrowing it.

HENRY. What?

RUBY. I'll fix the cover back on and everything. You gotta loan me that alcohol to clean out the insides first. *(Ruby holds out various pieces of a disassembled radio.)*

HENRY. Is that my Zenith? That's my Zenith! My parents gave me that when I made Dean's List. What'd you do to it?

RUBY. Looked at it.

HENRY. It's in pieces.

RUBY. Looked inside.

HENRY. Boy, I hope you never look inside me.

RUBY. It'll be back brand new soon as I'm done.

HENRY. Done with what?

RUBY. I said I'll return it.

HENRY. No, done with what? What's going on?

RUBY. On where?

HENRY. Out there in that barn.

RUBY. What about it?

HENRY. Here we are, living under the same roof; is it so strange to want to know something?

RUBY. I don't know you neither.

HENRY. Grew up in West Baden. My father runs a Feed and Dry Goods. My mother's a saint. I got six sisters, each of them married already. I could tell you about our swimming hole.

RUBY. Don't.

HENRY. So then you gotta tell me something about who *you* are. *(Pause.)*

RUBY. You ever hear people say the word Television?

HENRY. What word?

RUBY. Television. It means seeing things that are far away through your radio.

HENRY. What are you talking about?

RUBY. Electromagnetic radiation.

HENRY. What what?

RUBY. Energy in the form of waves. Radio — like how the songs on the radio travel over miles to get to you — is just one example. Light, the kind of light you see, that's another. In radio — okay? — music, or speech, whatever you hear, it's just vibrational patterns, converted into a different form of pattern: electromagnetic radiation. That way it can flow from the transmitter at the station to the radio receiver.

HENRY. What do you mean receiver?

RUBY. That's the radio, like your Zenith. The receiver converts the radio waves back into sound by vibrating a membrane, called the speaker. Television aims to work similar, 'cept it's seeking to reproduce visual patterns of dark and light, rather than just sound.

HENRY. Where'd you learn to talk like that?

RUBY. Like what?

HENRY. Membrane.

RUBY. My daddy.

HENRY. But he wasn't an engineer. Miss Haver said you grew up on a farm like me.

RUBY. I said he didn't have a degree. And besides, it was rightly my mamma who gave me lots of technical magazines: *Science and Invention, Popular Mechanics*.

HENRY. I thought you said your mamma died giving birth to you.

RUBY. Not right in birth. Not exactly right then.

HENRY. After.

RUBY. Uh huh, a little after.

HENRY. When you were old enough to read magazines. *(Pause.)*

RUBY. Can I take that liquor now like you said was okay?

HENRY. Wait.

RUBY. What?

HENRY. Just explain it all again one more time.

Scene 4

Ruby and Henry in the Barn. Morning. Ruby has set up an ad-hoc work space. There is a table fitted with several ring-stands with clamps. Wires have been diverted from the generator to a wooden framed box.

HENRY. You ever done this before?

RUBY. Partly. *(Ruby holds up a meshed metal screen with a wire ring around it.)* 'Kay, this is the cathode. Here's where the light rays get converted to an electron image. The first step is we gotta get the cathode stuck into one of those glass tube blanks that you borrowed from the University. The heavy wires are the leads.

HENRY. The leads.

RUBY. You gotta seal the leads through the wall of the tube, glass to metal.

HENRY. Uh huh. *(Ruby secures the cathode in a pair of forceps and hands it to Henry.)*

RUBY. Get a firm hold. *(She steadies the tube blank.)* Now slip it in.

HENRY. Slip it in?

RUBY. The cathode. I guess about a half-inch from the end.

HENRY. You're asking me?

RUBY. Half an inch. *(Henry inserts the cathode into the opening in the glass tube.)*

RUBY. Good. Don't move. *(Ruby lifts a torch and sets the flame going.)*

HENRY. *(Jerking away.)* Hey now.

RUBY. Just do what I tell you.

HENRY. But, careful. *(Ruby applies the flame to the tube.)*

RUBY. I gotta get the glass softened before you push the wire right on through.

HENRY. Through what?

RUBY. The glass.

HENRY. Don't get sore.

RUBY. I gotta switch to a hotter flame.

HENRY. Hotter? *(Ruby takes another torch, gets it going and applies it to the glass.)*

RUBY. The lighter flame is for starting and again at the end in order to prevent strains. Strain causes cracks, and we'll get one of these things blowing up in our face.

HENRY. It will?

RUBY. See that red dot forming?

HENRY. Is that bad?

RUBY. It means we're in business. You ready?

HENRY. If you are.

RUBY. Do it. *(Henry slides the wire through the molten spot on the tube.)*

HENRY. *(Excited.)* Oh hell, excuse my language.

RUBY. Straighten it a little? Yeah, flat like that. *(Henry does.)* It's in.

HENRY. Like that? *(Ruby changes back to the cooler flame and bathes the whole tube.)*

RUBY. Now hold still for god's sake while I cool it down.

HENRY. I'm still.

RUBY. You're shaking.

HENRY. I'm still as I get. *(Ruby turns off the flame. Beat.)*

RUBY. I think it's cooled.

HENRY. Yeah?

RUBY. Yeah. *(Ruby takes the newly made cathode from Henry and sets it down.)* That was good.

HENRY. That was great.

RUBY. I get the air pumped out and I'll have my first genuine prototype.

HENRY. Whatta you think of that? I made a photo-cathode tube. Well, we did. But you couldn't've done it alone.

RUBY. Suppose not.

HENRY. Now what?

RUBY. We gotta capture an image — it's gonna take a lot of light, get some more bulbs set up in here — but once we do, we can try sending it over the wires to the receiver.

HENRY. I thought you said the picture would move through the air.

RUBY. It will. But for the testing stage, it doesn't matter how it travels, just that it does, and that it seems like an unbroken image at the other end even though it's not.

HENRY. Why does it seem in a way it's not?

RUBY. 'Cause of your eye.

HENRY. My eye?

RUBY. The human eye retains an image on its retina for about less than a tenth of a second. That's called by Persistence of Vision. See, Television doesn't have to show a continuous picture. It replaces each and every line that makes up the image in less than that fraction of time. *(Holding up the cathode.)* That's why we need to coat these cathodes with something that can blink on and turn off. When the electrons light up the phosphorescent dots on the receiving end, your brain can assemble all that into a steady picture 'cause of how the vision persists.

HENRY. *(Looking at the cathode tube.)* What's that?

RUBY. I told you: Persistence of Vision is just …

HENRY. No, that.

RUBY. What's what?

HENRY. That line. That break supposed to be there? *(Ruby looks at the glass tube.)*

RUBY. There's a crack.

HENRY. That's what I …

RUBY. I heard you now.

HENRY. Oh, Ruby.

RUBY. It's worthless. *(She throws the tube against the wall. It shatters.)*

HENRY. Hey, don't do that. *(Ruby moves away from Henry to the barn door. Henry follows her.)* You're sad. Don't be sad. *(Silence. Ruby is looking out at the night.)* I hate it when you're sad. *(Silence.)* You'll get it next time. *(Silence.)* Besides, all those wires and stopcocks, no wonder it busted, it looks like something most awful stupid.

RUBY. It is not stupid. You're the one what's stupid.

HENRY. Got you talking.

RUBY. Don't much want to talk about it. Gotta think about it: what went wrong. *(Long silence.)*

HENRY. Look: fairies.

RUBY. What?

HENRY. Fairies out there. *(Ruby looks out.)*

RUBY. Fireflies.

HENRY. I know. How do they do it?

RUBY. What?

HENRY. Glow like that.

RUBY. Bioluminescence.

HENRY. You got a word for everything.

RUBY. Science has words.

HENRY. It looks nice anyhow. Like fairies making magic.

RUBY. It's a chemical process. Any living thing that glows has a substance inside it whose energy is increased 'cause of a chemical reaction. Then when it's returned to its original level, the substance inside the insect gets rid of the added energy and does it as light, gives off light. It makes the males and females find each other. *(Henry kisses her. He pulls back.)*

HENRY. I'm sorry. I interrupted you.

RUBY. Mnnnhmmm.

HENRY. Can I do it again?

RUBY. You mean, right now?

HENRY. Yeah. I mean, are you finished?

RUBY. Finished? I'm not finished.

HENRY. But with the fireflies. You were explaining about light.

RUBY. Sometimes it's a chemical process.

HENRY. Uh huh.

RUBY. I gotta get back to work.

HENRY. You mean, right now?

RUBY. Yeah. *(Pause.)* You're interested in fireflies.

HENRY. I sure am, Ruby.

RUBY. Because maybe you could borrow me some potassium hydride from the lab at your school. It releases energy, too.

HENRY. Some what?

RUBY. I'll write it down for you. They're bound to have it in the lab.

HENRY. I don't even take chemistry.

RUBY. Fireflies. It's like fireflies. *(And they kiss more.)*

Scene 5

The Kitchen. Lois sits at the table with a bottle. Henry enters.

LOIS. You're up late.

HENRY. Could say same to you.

LOIS. How'd that exam fare you?

HENRY. Fine.

LOIS. You're gonna be finished soon, huh? I'll be so proud when you get that degree even though I'll miss you something terrible. Never find another boarder like you.

HENRY. G'night, Miss Haver.

LOIS. *(Seeing his face.)* Oh my lord, you got a shiner coming.

HENRY. Big deal.

LOIS. And been drinking; smell your breath.

HENRY. Smell yours.

LOIS. That's different. You sit down.

HENRY. Don't wanna. *(Lois sits him down.)* Owww.

LOIS. For your own good. *(She gets a cold cloth and cleans his eye.)* Now tell me all about it.

HENRY. Nothing to tell.

LOIS. Who socked you?

HENRY. I socked him back.

LOIS. And you're proud of that? It's not like you.

HENRY. A bunch of the kids got together out by Webber's field. I invited Ruby to come along.

LOIS. Ruby.

HENRY. All the fellows were bringing girls. But she's right away brushing me off. What's the point of sitting in a field, she says. Why would I want to do that? I say, what's the point of sitting in a barn? She says, go then, by yourself, go on. I'm so mad. First thing someone says about my mystery girl doesn't exist ... next thing I know they're dragging us apart.

LOIS. Ruby is your girl now?

HENRY. I don't know. How can she be my girl when all she wants me to do is stick wires everyplace?

LOIS. You aren't being stupid, are you? Two kids your age …

HENRY. What difference does it make?

LOIS. A big difference if you're being stupid. You'll wind up with a big difference nine months from now.

HENRY. I could have any girl in West Baden. Soon as I finish my degree. But I'm yearning after one who'd rather be messing in a barn on something that won't ever do nothing as far as I can tell than holding my hand in front of my friends. It hurts. Everyone sees it. And all the world knows that I am not worth loving.

LOIS. There, there.

HENRY. I mean what's she doing? What's she doing out there right this minute?

LOIS. Nonsense is what, and don't say I didn't warn you. You know what they used to call her? The Crazy Girl from Kokomo. Oooh, she hated that. The Crazy Crazy Girl. *(She re-applies the cloth to his face.)*

HENRY. Stop it.

LOIS. The cool'll take the swelling down.

HENRY. I said get off.

LOIS. Don't be silly.

HENRY. I'm not your boyfriend, Miss Haver. I'm your boarder. I pay you money.

LOIS. I know that.

HENRY. Just because your life was over a long time ago, doesn't mean mine has to be. *(Pause.)*

LOIS. I'm sorry, Henry.

HENRY. Oh gosh, I'm a dog. I'm all mixed up. I better go to bed before I break anything else stupid.

LOIS. Sure, you go on up to bed. Take this. *(Offering the cold cloth.)* If you want.

HENRY. Thank you, Miss Haver. I …

LOIS. Good night, Henry.

Scene 6

The Barn. Ruby's Television has grown. She is finishing up a demonstration for Lois.

RUBY. And the rest is a mere matter of dollars, cents, and guts. *(Pause. Lois walks around the contraption.)* Well, aren't you going to say something?
LOIS. Where'd you get all this stuff?
RUBY. Borrowed it.
LOIS. You borrowed a table? Borrowed a ... *(Having no words to describe what she sees.)* What is all this stuff?
RUBY. That there's a lens, took it off a bicycle lamp.
LOIS. Borrowed that, too, huh?
RUBY. It's how light from the image gets focused before it's amplified. Amplification's the hardest part. It's why it's been four months 'stead of two.
LOIS. 'Stead of two weeks.
RUBY. Right. But it's gonna be worth it.
LOIS. Worth what?
RUBY. How Television's gonna change people. Make a whole different world where people can see the world right in their own homes. Moving pictures in your living room. You'll get to watch a home run sitting in your favorite chair, see the news as it's happening. 'Cause if I can broadcast a single point of light from here to there, then anyone can broadcast the bunch of points of light that make up an image, and send it as far as they care to. Soon, we'll get pictures from all over the world, and learn about our comrades in other countries, hell, other planets. If we could see their faces, we'd understand them better, and all our differences could be settled around tables, instead of going to war. Television will be the end of war 'cause who could bear it? Who could bear to see war right in your own living room?
LOIS. What do you know about war? You were just a kid then.
RUBY. Right, just a kid and I had to live through all that.
LOIS. That's your excuse for stealing light bulbs?
RUBY. Television'll make for better people, Aunt Lois.
LOIS. Better people: you sound like a Red.

21

RUBY. What's so bad about better?

LOIS. You "borrow" my home brew, too, Miss Sunrise?

RUBY. A little maybe.

LOIS. Care to offer me a glass of my own stock? *(Ruby takes a bottle that's hidden away and offers it to Lois.)*

RUBY. It was almost empty already before.

LOIS. You want some?

RUBY. No, ma'am, I don't use it for that.

LOIS. For what?

RUBY. I use it for my equipment.

LOIS. Not to forget about your daddy?

RUBY. No, not like that.

LOIS. 'Cause that's what I use it for. Forget all about that day in church when I first saw him: a face so sweet like the sun kept kissing him.

RUBY. Guess the sun went behind a cloud.

LOIS. Sure did. Made me wish he was dead. You ever wish he was dead?

RUBY. I'm not sure what you're asking me.

LOIS. I got a telephone call, Ruby. Now either they're stretching the wires down to Hades these days, or your daddy's alive and well and walking around on earth.

RUBY. You don't have a telephone.

LOIS. Telephone up at the post office.

RUBY. Must've been a mistake.

LOIS. I don't like liars.

RUBY. Mnnnhmmm.

LOIS. Did he beat you, Ruby?

RUBY. Mnnnhmmm.

LOIS. Son of a bitch.

RUBY. What'd he want?

LOIS. He wants you home.

RUBY. No.

LOIS. He's your daddy, Ruby.

RUBY. No.

LOIS. He's got rights to claim you.

RUBY. He'll destroy it, Aunt Lois. All over again. I was barely getting started in Kokomo. I had my laboratory — and I was doing my chores all the same, I swear I was — but he would get mean drunk, worse than when my mamma was alive, and you know how he used to do her. You saw her face when we came here.

LOIS. You were too young then, to remember that.

RUBY. When she got sick, it stopped for a while. But after she died … I don't even mind the hits; he can smack me all he wants, scream at me. But my equipment. My lab in pieces. My notes in the fire. Don't make me go back there.

LOIS. An unmarried girl has got to do what her father says.

RUBY. What's that supposed to mean?

LOIS. You're saying you don't want to go back to Kokomo? I'm saying I bet Henry'll be pleased to hear it.

RUBY. Unmarried girl.

LOIS. It's what he wants.

RUBY. But what if I don't want it?

LOIS. That boy cares for you. A whole lot.

RUBY. I know, and it's slowing me down.

LOIS. Slowing *you* down? He hasn't cracked a book of his own studies in a month.

RUBY. 'Cause this is more interesting, more important than how many oats to feed your cattle to get the fat ratio right.

LOIS. Don't be smart. I'm offering you something here. It rips my heart all over again, and still I'm offering it.

RUBY. Yes, ma'am.

LOIS. And I want you to stop lying. And stop stealing my liquor.

RUBY. Yes, ma'am.

LOIS. Now, you think about it, Ruby. Lots of girls would be happy for a chance like this.

RUBY. I am thinking, Aunt Lois. All I do is think.

Scene 7

The Barn. Ruby is working on her Television, connecting the wires in a circuit which links the transmitter, the receiver, and the generator. Henry enters. He stands by the barn door for a moment before Ruby sees him.

RUBY. Hey. I thought you were at the library.

HENRY. I was.

RUBY. Don't you have a final tomorrow?

HENRY. Yeah.

RUBY. Well, Mr. Dean's List, what are you doing back here?

HENRY. Quit.

RUBY. What?

HENRY. Quit messing with the wires for once. *(She looks up from her equipment.)*

RUBY. What happened to you?

HENRY. I took a break. When I was studying. I went to the news-papers.

RUBY. Okay.

HENRY. They had *The New York Times.*

RUBY. Okay, *The New York Times.*

HENRY. Ruby, they already did it.

RUBY. Did what?

HENRY. What you're doing. It's done.

RUBY. Nobody's doing what I'm doing.

HENRY. You're wrong. *(He pulls out a piece of paper.)* I wrote it down on account of how I knew you wouldn't trust my word. *(Reading.)* "Far-off Speakers Seen as Well as Heard in a Test of Television."

RUBY. What are you talking about?

HENRY. *(Still reading.)* "Like a Photo Come to Life. Hoover's Face Plainly Imaged as He Speaks in Washington." *(Looking up.)* The American Telegraph and Telephone Company, they did it. The Paper explained how and everything. *(Reading.)* "Dots of light are put together at a rate of forty-five thousand a second ... " *(Looking up.)* And like that. I couldn't get it all down. I'll take you tomor-row. It seems this fellow Dr. Ives ...

RUBY. Who?

HENRY. Ives, he's a doctor. *(From the paper.)* And R.C. Mathes ... *(Ruby begins to laugh.)*

HENRY. Or Maths. Matheez, I guess. Why are you laughing?

RUBY. Oh my god, oh god.

HENRY. What?

RUBY. Henry, it's okay; it doesn't matter.

HENRY. They did it. They made a Television. It's over.

RUBY. Ives and Gray are still working with spinning wooden disks. I read their report eight months ago. It's nothing. Bet the picture was for diddley-squat. What was it: two inches wide?

HENRY. Two by three, it said.

RUBY. Inches. Inches, Henry. Would you go to the the-ater if it

24

was two inches big?

HENRY. By three. And they showed it on a bigger screen, too.

RUBY. It must've looked like hell, all white spots and smudges.

HENRY. It said it was a little unclear.

RUBY. Even they admit that to get a four by four inch picture, they're gonna need a six foot diameter disk. You want a six foot thing spinning in your living room?

HENRY. But they beat you. You can stop now.

RUBY. I'm not making this up. American Telegraph is trying to do it mechanically.

HENRY. *The New York Times* says …

RUBY. *The New York Times, The New York Times*, I can say it, too; it don't make it holy. The picture is for squat. I don't need some fancy paper to tell me that. Why don't you have the guts to say that you just don't think I can do it, instead of parading some trash piece of paper like it's the news that's doubting me instead of you.

HENRY. Who the hell gets you those tubes, that wire? For crying out loud, every piece of crap in here came from me whether I bought it or stole it, sorry, "borrowed" it. I did all that.

RUBY. You want it back? You want your share of the investment?

HENRY. Aww, stop it.

RUBY. I buy you out, here and now, you're bought out, I'll pay you back every cent as soon as I file and my patent clears. And when people say my name, you'll be sorry then.

HENRY. Nobody's gonna be saying your name.

RUBY. What do you know? How could I expect you to understand?

HENRY. That phony contraption isn't ever gonna do what you say.

RUBY. Nobody believed Marconi either, but he didn't stop.

HENRY. It's too late, Ruby. What's it gonna take for you to quit this nonsense?

RUBY. Ignorant cattle farmer.

HENRY. Crazy Girl from Kokomo. *(For a moment Ruby stops her work, stops moving.)*

RUBY. Get out.

HENRY. I'm sorry.

RUBY. Get out of my laboratory. I'm working. *(She goes back to adjusting the wires.)*

HENRY. Miss Haver let it slip one night. I'm sorry.

RUBY. I don't need any of you.

HENRY. Put down the wires for a minute. I love you. I want to do what's right. Two people who've done what we've done ought to do what's right.

RUBY. Don't come one step closer.

HENRY. What's wrong with that? That's normal. We've known each other.

RUBY. I said, stop.

HENRY. I know the truth about your daddy. I was waiting for you to come clean yourself. *(Ruby begins to prime the generator.)*

RUBY. I'm not hearing a thing you're saying.

HENRY. I know he's coming here. Soon.

RUBY. I'm not listening.

HENRY. I'm saying … Ruby, will you marry me? *(As Ruby gets the generator turning, something shorts. Ruby is thrown across the barn with an electrical shock and slams to the floor. The entire circuit of the TV system sizzles and fumes. The electric lights pop out. Ruby's body is shaking. Henry rushes to her.)* Are you okay? Ruby, honey, are you okay?

RUBY. My baby.

HENRY. *(Realizing what she means.)* Oh my god.

End of Part One

PART TWO

Scene 1

New York City, 1952. The office of TV producer Martin Marcus. The writer Tad Rose sits with Martin, who has a copy of Variety in front of him.

MARTIN. Goddamnit. Goddamnit.
TAD. Nobody reads *Variety*.
MARTIN. My employers read *Variety*. Goddamnit. *(Throwing the* Variety *down.)* Whose shitheel idea was it to do *The Sea Battle of Bismark*? Stupid model ship bobbing up and down like one of my kid's bath toys.
TAD. Naval warfare is popular in the movies, Martin.
MARTIN. This is Television. Tele-Vision. That's Latin for Simple-Story.
TAD. I don't think it's Latin.
MARTIN. Latin, Greek, it's not American. All I know is sponsors are jumping like rats, and the boys upstairs want my slot for a variety show.
TAD. Not another variety show.
MARTIN. Or wrestling. They say the box can't sustain narrative, who needs another narrative in their living room.
TAD. What, the Philco Goodyear Playhouse isn't narrative?
MARTIN. Sure, flaunt the competition in my face; twist the knife a little deeper.
TAD. *Bismark* wasn't your fault.
MARTIN. Can I blame the writer?
TAD. Don't blame the writer. The problem was the girl can't act.
MARTIN. The problem is never the-girl-can't-act. Who expects Suzie Tyrone to act? She looks good wet. *(Lulu enters.)*
LULU. Morning, Mr. Marcus, here's your coffee.
MARTIN. Miss Miles, what are you doing bringing the coffee? Where's Mitzie?

27

LULU. She's here. It's just Allan Wright is visiting Studio Four.

MARTIN. Oh, Allan Wright, heavens forbid I would deprive any girl of a vision of Allan Wright. *(As she sets the coffee down.)* Allan Wright doesn't interest you?

LULU. Between you and me?

MARTIN. And the furniture. And Mr. Rose here.

LULU. Tad Rose?

TAD. How do you do?

LULU. Mr. Rose, I thought *Return to Morgan Hill* was the finest play I've ever seen on Television. I'm sorry; I'm gushing.

TAD. No; thank you.

MARTIN. He detests praise.

TAD. Although I think you're alone in your esteemed opinion.

MARTIN. Mr. Rose is going to be writing something for us, pronto; isn't that right, Tad?

TAD. Talk to my agent.

LULU. That's wonderful news.

TAD. I'll say.

MARTIN. First script I bought off this joker he didn't have an agent. Walked it here himself and put it in Flo's in-box.

LULU. That's the way to do it.

MARTIN. That's how he did it. Too bad he forgot to put his name on the thing, no less an address where we could reach him.

TAD. No one wants to hear this story, Martin.

MARTIN. But it's legendary: The true tale of how Tad Rose stopped selling appliances for a living.

LULU. You sold appliances?

TAD. Distant, distant past.

MARTIN. Dinosaurs roaming. Cavemen.

TAD. That type of thing.

LULU. If there's anything I can do to assist you, it would be an honor. I do more than fetch coffee.

MARTIN. Mr. Rose doesn't drink coffee since his nervous breakdown.

TAD. I do drink coffee.

LULU. Would you like a cup?

MARTIN. You arrogant son of a bitch, Miss Miles is my new script coordinator, fresh off the boat from Indiana ...

TAD. Boat?

LULU. Fresh?

MARTIN. ... my script coordinator, not your secretary.

TAD. I didn't ask for coffee.

LULU. I'd be pleased to.

TAD. *(Rising.)* I'm on my way out.

LULU. Are you sure? It's raining out there.

TAD. Thank you, no.

MARTIN. I want something in my hand the next time I see you. *(Tad exits.)*

LULU. That's a lot of pressure to put on the guy.

MARTIN. I had to light a fire under him. I've got a slot in two weeks.

LULU. What happened to Joey McCorkle's project?

MARTIN. Adultery and alcoholics. Continuity Acceptance will crawl so far up my ass before they approve that shit. I told Joey, patch things up with the wife and get me something when you're sober.

LULU. Did Mr. Rose pitch a play?

MARTIN. He said he had a hundred ideas which is writer talk for none. You have those readers' reports for me?

LULU. I don't.

MARTIN. You don't.

LULU. Mr. Marcus, I didn't even want to waste your time. *Pride and Prejudice* is not a book that makes for a teleplay.

MARTIN. Philco's killing us with the class acts.

LULU. There's more to classy material than rich people in mansions talking in high-class accents. There are stories to tell about the little guy, an American guy, and the contributions they make; or even fail to make. You see a bum on the street, or a woman yelling at her kids after working in a factory all day, but to really understand what causes that behavior … Each of these people had goals; they had dreams; they had disappointments. TV can get inside that, can get close, and be honest about it. That's what's classy.

MARTIN. So no more period pieces?

LULU. If they're topical.

MARTIN. Pride and prejudice: sounds topical.

LULU. It's about marriage. Today's audience has more on their mind than who marries who. *(Tad enters.)*

TAD. Excuse me.

LULU. Mr. Rose.

TAD. My umbrella.

MARTIN. You should stay and take notes. Miss Miles is telling us about today's audience.

LULU. I wouldn't presume to tell Mr. Rose what subject matter to address in his writing.

TAD. Please call me Tad.

MARTIN. She calls me Mr. Marcus.

LULU. You're a married man.

MARTIN. How do you know he's not married?

LULU. I don't.

TAD. You can call me Tad.

LULU. *(Handing it to him.)* Your umbrella.

TAD. Thank you.

MARTIN. Two weeks. *(Tad exits.)*

Scene 2

A coffee shop. Tad sits, drinking coffee, soup in front of him. Lulu enters and approaches.

LULU. You weren't lying. You do drink coffee.

TAD. Miss Miles. *(She sits with him.)*

LULU. Aren't you curious about my first name?

TAD. Lulu. Short for Lois. But no one calls you Lois.

LULU. Quite curious.

TAD. Mitzie loves to gossip.

LULU. And what was the gossip?

TAD. She didn't have much. Evidently, you display a very professional demeanor.

LULU. You dug around.

TAD. I'm a writer.

LULU. That explains it. Did Mitzie tell you she thinks Allan Wright has a funny nose?

TAD. Then why'd she hit Studio Four?

LULU. She didn't. I lied.

TAD. You're a liar?

LULU. When I have a worthy agenda. It runs in the family.

TAD. What's a worthy agenda?

LULU. Something you're trying to accomplish that you believe in desperately. What do you think a worthy agenda is?

TAD. I meant what's your worthy agenda?

LULU. Well, for the immediate, I wanted the opportunity to meet you, so I engineered it to have Mitzie occupied with a movie star at coffee time.

TAD. You brought Martin coffee so you could meet me?

LULU. Brewed it myself.

TAD. I ... don't know what to say.

LULU. I'm sure if you try, you can come up with something.

TAD. All I can think right now is Allan Wright's given name is Hiram Markowitz. That might account for the funny nose.

LULU. But aren't you Jewish?

TAD. Is that a problem?

LULU. Are you asking me out on a date?

TAD. If I were ... would it be a problem?

LULU. I'm a bastard from the mid-west; is that a problem?

TAD. Are you equating Jews and bastards?

LULU. Yes, I'll accept a date with you. Does that answer your Jewish question? Tad.

TAD. My mother named me Tad.

LULU. A likely story.

TAD. Are you free tomorrow night?

LULU. Tomorrow night? I thought you were sweating under a deadline.

TAD. Am I speaking to the attractive young woman who sought me out in my favorite coffee shop, or to Martin Marcus's script girl?

LULU. Same person. That's the catch. How's the soup?

TAD. Watery.

LULU. Fifty-three minutes of material with so few days to write it. I can't imagine how you people do it.

TAD. Which people?

LULU. Writers.

TAD. We resign ourselves to the fact that each project is an extended sales pitch for the sponsor; that takes the pressure off.

LULU. Baloney. You forget I've seen your work. I've seen you take on some real topics.

TAD. Recently?

LULU. *(Considering.)* Recently ...

TAD. Everyone's a critic.

LULU. I'm not; I'm a fan. I know what you're capable of.

TAD. But failing to deliver.

LULU. I didn't say that. Are you saying that?

TAD. Do you have any idea what it feels like to sit in a rehearsal

— that's if they let you into rehearsal — most of the time, they shut you out, god forbid you should have an opinion about the thing you created — and you sit there watching your script get cut by ad execs, mangled by the director, butchered by the actors ...

LULU. I was under the impression that you'd worked with some of our finest actors.

TAD. Actors, as a breed, are the least realistic people alive; and somehow they're encouraged to re-write my dialogue on "instinct." You have to learn not to care: It'll only get you ulcers.

LULU. Your cynicism is charming; but I know better than to buy it.

TAD. Better based on what?

LULU. *Return to Morgan Hill.*

TAD. Which is exactly where I learned my lesson. The reviewers shredded me on that one.

LULU. Forget the reviewers. The reviewers don't know how an aspiring script girl sat in a bar with a girlfriend on a Sunday night, and convinced seven, inebriated wrestling fans to turn to the other channel; and I'm telling you, every one of those drunks had tuned in by the end, and I guarantee they thought differently from that day forward about their fellow workers, and their wives. You made a meaningful event, and I know because I shared it among strangers in a smoke-filled bar.

TAD. You didn't have a TV at home?

LULU. No. We were poor.

TAD. So were we, but as soon as the cheap, well, cheap-er, ones started coming out ...

LULU. My mother would never allow a Television in her house.

TAD. That sounds definitive.

LULU. It was. The point is lots of people appreciate your work, Tad; I saw it with my own eyes.

TAD. "Lots of people" don't write the paychecks.

LULU. But they do. In the long run, they do.

TAD. I'm too out of shape for the long run. Look, I'm sorry to be downbeat — and god forbid the girl doesn't marry the boy at the end because you're forever branded "downbeat" — but at two hundred and fifty a script, Martin doesn't pay me enough to talk about work after seven.

LULU. All right. Let's talk about me.

TAD. The Middle West, you said?

LULU. Indianapolis.

TAD. Right, a hoosier. You miss your family?

LULU. Bastard and now orphan: My mother passed. And I never met my father.

TAD. I'm sorry.

LULU. About which one?

TAD. That just must be hard.

LULU. Hard, yes.

TAD. But you made it here.

LULU. As fast as I could.

TAD. How does a poor girl from Indiana make her way to the big bad city?

LULU. You're interested?

TAD. Deeply.

LULU. A man capable of "deeply."

TAD. Do you drink, Miss Miles?

LULU. Only after seven, Mr. Rose.

TAD. It just so happens we find ourselves in that time slot.

LULU. What a coincidence.

Scene 3

Martin's Office. Tad enters. Martin leaps from behind his desk and kisses him.

MARTIN. Fantastic. We love it. If the second act is anything like the first, we've got a hit and *Variety* can kiss my Yiddish ass.

TAD. Settle down, Marty.

MARTIN. The script is perfection. Where did you come up with this idea? And the detail.

TAD. That's why you pay me three hundred and fifty a pop.

MARTIN. Two fifty; nice try. But after this gets on, maybe we can ask for more.

TAD. Maybe.

MARTIN. Wasn't so long ago you were selling door-to-door. *(Martin picks up the phone.)* Mitzie, would you get Miss Miles? *(To Tad.)* I want her in on these script change notes.

TAD. Perfection needs alterations?

MARTIN. Do yourself a favor and lose the smartass. Miss Miles is the best mind I've encountered since I started in this racket.

TAD. It's like she was born to do it.

MARTIN. Let's not get philosophical.

TAD. Has Miss Miles read the script? *(Lulu enters.)*

LULU. She has.

MARTIN. Miss Miles, you remember Mr. ... oh yes, Tad.

LULU. Mr. Oh-Yes-Tad, surely I do.

MARTIN. Miss Miles had a lot of nice ideas about your script.

TAD. You liked it okay?

LULU. It's a good story.

TAD. I was pretty sure you'd either love it or hate it.

LULU. It had a familiar ring. I won't make a secret of that.

TAD. You don't keep secrets?

LULU. I do when asked. Even implicitly.

TAD. Good to know.

LULU. It's important that this story's being told. We just have to be certain we tell it accurately.

MARTIN. I thought it was fiction.

LULU and TAD. It is.

MARTIN. Jinx. Who owes me a Coca Cola?

LULU. It's fictional, but it speaks to the truth; that's why Tad is so brilliant.

MARTIN. What about me, I hired him?

LULU. You're the most brilliant of all.

MARTIN. Glad we got that straight. Now first off, right off the bat ... what do we have, Miss Miles?

LULU. *(Reading from her notes.)* Bastard, page 6, twice on page 12, page 20, and again on 32.

MARTIN. Right, if you're using it to mean a child born out of wedlock ...

LULU. Page 19.

MARTIN. But for the rest ... you understand. *(Continuing.)* Miss Miles.

LULU. Son of a bitch, page 11. Comrade, page 30.

TAD. Comrade?

LULU. Mr. Marcus pointed out that it might lead to unintended interpretations.

MARTIN. It's not a good time for comrade.

TAD. Jesus.

MARTIN. Friend. Why not friend? Who the hell uses the word comrade?

TAD. Are you asking me a loaded question?

MARTIN. Do not even fuck with me for one minute on this communist crap. I had to sign a loyalty oath myself, Miss Miles had to sign one — which reminds me, Miss Miles, they called from upstairs, they didn't get your oath on file.

LULU. Really?

MARTIN. They're sending down another one.

LULU. Okay.

MARTIN. We had to sign oaths, Tad, and we might not have liked it, but there it is. Don't force me into a difficult position.

TAD. *(An oath.)* Am not now. Have never been.

MARTIN. *(Continuing.)* Miss Miles.

LULU. And too many instances of Jesus, Jesus Christ, goddamn, goddamnit, and other variations to mention.

TAD. It's a heated story and a feisty character.

LULU. We want to make it beautiful.

MARTIN. We want to make it saleable.

LULU. And no premarital sex.

TAD. Excuse me?

LULU. In the script.

MARTIN. Oh, yeah, I had an idea on this one, to simplify the change. We don't want to fuck with your words; you're the writer.

TAD. Here it comes.

MARTIN. So how about before the commercial break when the Ruby girl says, "My baby," I thought, why not let that refer to the TV instead of to her pregnancy?

LULU. That's a great idea.

TAD. What are you talking about?

MARTIN. Well, we discussed ... *(Turning to Lulu for help.)* Miss Miles?

LULU. We discussed how driven she is, this character, and how she probably cares more about her new invention than she could ever care about a child.

MARTIN. Yes, that was it.

TAD. She cared about her child. How could she not care about her child?

MARTIN. That's gorgeous talk, and we'll use it someday, but this time around, for the sake of Continuity Acceptance, let's smooth out some of the crags and avoid that particular poetry by saying she's not, in fact, pregnant.

TAD. But the pregnancy's a major part of where the play's headed.

LULU. It doesn't have to be.

MARTIN. If we want to see this broadcast to six million homes, we've got to play ball with Continuity Acceptance.

TAD. Continuity Acceptance. It would stick in my craw less if they'd go ahead and call it "The Censorship Office."

MARTIN. I'm sure Jerry will find a way to keep the heat in the story alive.

TAD. Jerry Ritt?

MARTIN. Oh, you like Jerry Ritt? Finally, we get a rise out of this guy.

TAD. He would do Television?

LULU. If he's directing Elizabeth Hunter as Ruby he would.

TAD. Hot damn.

LULU. She's perfect. I know, she's perfect.

MARTIN. Don't let's get ahead of ourselves. We've got a call in to her agent. But Jerry's in. The first act sold him. Plus he owes me.

TAD. Okay, okay, so we soften the pregnancy. Ruby Sunrise goes off at the end of the play to ... I'll think of something.

LULU. I'm sure you will.

MARTIN. And maybe she doesn't have to go off: Would it be so terrible if she marries the nice farmer boy? You don't want to be downbeat.

LULU. We want Tad to get his vision across.

TAD. Thank you; I agree with everything Miss Miles says.

LULU. Thank you; you're very wise to say so.

MARTIN. Is the festival of praise over? I talk with Jerry tomorrow. Reading Wednesday. *(The phone rings a quick double ring.)* If we're going with *The Ruby Sunrise*, we've got to move, move. *(Picks up the phone.)* Yeah? *(Listens.)* Oh Christ. Tell him to sit down. I hear you, Mitzie. Give him coffee, black. *(He hangs up.)* Joey McCorkle's in the lobby.

LULU. I'll take it.

MARTIN. Thanks, hon. *(Lulu rises and moves to the door.)*

TAD. Good-bye, Lulu.

LULU. Good luck, Tad. *(Lulu exits. Martin looks at Tad, grinning. A beat.)*

TAD. What?

MARTIN. Best mind I've ever encountered: as if I need to be telling you.

TAD. Telling me what?

MARTIN. What else is she "born" to do?

TAD. Who?

MARTIN. Give me a break: I see the score here. Miss Miles is like a daughter to me.

TAD. What are you asking, Martin?

MARTIN. Does she fuck?

TAD. Oh, for Chrissakes.

MARTIN. Come on, does she?

TAD. How would I know? Dad. *(Lulu enters.)*

LULU. I'm sorry to interrupt. What *did* I interrupt?

TAD AND MARTIN. Nothing.

LULU. Who owes me a Coca Cola?

MARTIN. What gives with McCorkle?

LULU. He wants to talk to *you.*

MARTIN. He said that?

LULU. He said he wants to talk to "someone who matters."

MARTIN. Tell him to go home and come back when he's appropriate.

LULU. I did.

TAD. Good for you.

LULU. And he said he wants to talk to someone who matters.

MARTIN. I'll go put him out on his ear. Will you attend to Miss Miles?

LULU. I haven't been damaged.

MARTIN. Be right back. *(Martin exits.)*

LULU. Thus proving the point.

TAD. What point?

LULU. That I am not someone who matters.

TAD. That McCorkle is a drunk is the only thing that's been proved. Thanks for not divulging my, uh, inspiration. I was desperate to come in with something, and I had a hundred ideas, but nothing seemed to work.

LULU. I won't tell Mr. Marcus if you don't. Not that he'd care where the story came from, as long as it's good; and Ruby's good.

TAD. Why didn't you ever tell anyone before me?

LULU. Maybe none of them was the right guy. Some secrets, you need to know they'll stay secret.

TAD. But why?

LULU. It's hard enough for a lady to find work in this business without everyone thinking she has an axe to grind.

TAD. Do you have an axe?

LULU. It doesn't need grinding.

TAD. I should have asked before I started typing.

LULU. Don't worry about that. I had more than a hunch you might take a shine to my mother's story.

TAD. You've got me pegged, huh?

LULU. Not quite pegged; there's things I'm still finding out.

TAD. So what's next?

LULU. You mean after Ruby's prototype shorted? That's Act Two.

TAD. I mean after I take you out to a proper dinner.

LULU. That is also Act Two.

TAD. I'm looking forward to Act Two.

LULU. Aren't we all?

Intermission

Scene 4

An office. Tad and Lulu are working on the script.

LULU. What do you mean, no?

TAD. Because it can't be a fire.

LULU. Can't? It was.

TAD. A fire destroyed Ruby's lab?

LULU. It happened while she was still in bed, recovering from the electric shock.

TAD. You can't make a fire in a standard issue Television studio seven flights above Broadway. The Department of Buildings will close you down. The Fire Department. How about a flood? Throw some water around.

LULU. It doesn't flood outside of Indianapolis in May.

TAD. We call it September.

LULU. By September 1927 Philo T. Farnsworth had his all-electrical system going in San Francisco.

TAD. That's the Mormon guy?

LULU. Am I talking to the walls here?

TAD. What difference does it make, if the story's "fictional"?

LULU. It needs to operate within the facts that we all know.

TAD. But it's facts that nobody knows. Ask any stranger on the street who invented the Television, they couldn't care less.

LULU. But if you ignore actual events on the time line, you undermine her completely and once again the little guy's story doesn't get a chance. It's the big corporations writing history.

TAD. Martin will laugh me out of the office, I write a fire. Not even Jerry Ritt can make flames fly live.

LULU. If it's a flood, it makes it fate when Ruby's TV is destroyed. It wasn't her fate.

TAD. What was it then: her fault?

LULU. It wasn't her fault.

TAD. Whose fault was it?

LULU. Henry's.

TAD. What's Henry got to do with it?

LULU. How did you think the fire started? Her whole lab, all her equipment burned to the ground.

TAD. A bunch of leads hooked up to an old generator is how. It had already shorted once: We established that before the act break. And the cans of oil she used for cleaning the equipment.

LULU. No. Henry.

TAD. Henry what?

LULU. Started the fire.

TAD. But he loved her.

LULU. And hated her machine.

TAD. You know this for a fact?

LULU. I know what my mother told me, okay?

TAD. Have you ever asked Henry?

LULU. No, Tad, I've never asked him.

TAD. I'm sorry. *(Beat.)* Have you ever thought about trying to find him?

LULU. Did he ever think about trying to find me?

TAD. He might not even know you exist.

LULU. Perfect. I don't exist for him, and he doesn't exist for me.

TAD. It's different.

LULU. He's not my father, Tad. He's probably someone else's father. I'm sure he has the life he deserves now, with the prettiest wife in West Baden. Can we talk about the teleplay?

TAD. It's just too bad.

LULU. What is?

TAD. He was our likable college kid.

LULU. He still can be.

TAD. A likable arsonist: That'll go over big.

LULU. He didn't do it because he's a monster. He did it because it was the only way to insure that Ruby would marry him.

TAD. But she didn't marry him. She took a job in a textile mill.

LULU. He couldn't have known how strong her will would be.

TAD. I just don't buy it.

LULU. You weren't doubting my word when Act One showed up on Martin's desk.

TAD. I thought you called him Mr. Marcus.

LULU. If you want to steal someone's story, steal it whole.

TAD. Is that what this is about?

LULU. What?

TAD. Credit?

LULU. Don't be silly. I'm a script girl; I know that.

TAD. So why do you bother?

LULU. Don't tell me you bother just so you can see your name flicker on a screen for three seconds.

TAD. Five seconds. It's in my contract.

LULU. And creating something meaningful doesn't even cross your mind?

TAD. You heard Martin: People want a happy ending.

LULU. This is a happy ending.

TAD. A woman dies in obscurity from alcohol poisoning without ever having achieved her goals. Tell me how that's a happy ending.

LULU. It's like that phrase: Persistence of Vision. Sure, it's about the science, it means something technical, but it's more. There was a girl who ran away from what everyone expected from her, and from her persistence and her vision, she made something fantastic. Television!

TAD. You say that like you know what it means. We don't even know what it means yet.

LULU. I do know what it means. "Tele" is Greek for far and "vision" is Latin for seeing, and it's the perfect name, because it's democratic.

TAD. Democratic?

LULU. Yes, both languages get a vote. And what TV does is democratic: a machine that treats everyone equal, so a girl in Indiana is as important as a fat cat in New Jersey. TV is free. It moves through the air that we breathe. You don't have to buy a ticket. You don't need a car. We're all together even if we're a thousand miles apart. We all belong. Finally. Don't look at me like I'm crazy.

TAD. That's not how I'm looking at you.

LULU. How then?

TAD. Like you're beautiful.

LULU. Beautiful.

TAD. Martin called you a genius; do you know that? He says you have the best feel for Television of anyone he's ever met.

LULU. That doesn't mean he'll promote me. He said that?

TAD. He said more.

LULU. And what do you say?

TAD. I'm here, aren't I? With you, aren't I?

LULU. Yes, you are here with me.

TAD. Yes, I am. Here with you. *(Pause.)*

LULU. Do I scare you?

TAD. Yes, but why do you ask?

LULU. Because you still haven't tried to kiss me.

TAD. Do you want me to kiss you?

LULU. Do I have to answer that? *(She waits. He kisses her.)* Now we've got that out of the way.

TAD. I'm not sure that's out of the way.

LULU. A fire?

TAD. A blazing, booming, hot-as-hell fire.

LULU. Because I'm a genius? And I know how Ruby's story should be told?

TAD. A fire. *(And they kiss again.)*

Scene 5

The Rehearsal Hall. The actor Paul Benjamin (Henry from Part One) sits in a chair. He eats a sandwich as he reads a script. Martin enters.

PAUL. Morning, Mr. Marcus.

MARTIN. Paul. Glad you could join us.

PAUL. Thrilled to. It's one hell of a script. My agent only gave me Act One.

MARTIN. Yeah. You're the first one here.

PAUL. I'm still doing the voice for the canned beef so I was right around the corner.

MARTIN. That's going well for you.

PAUL. My agent said Elizabeth Hunter's doing the Ruby part. You know in summer stock …

MARTIN. Yeah, uh, Tad Rose, our writer, and the others should be here shortly. You need coffee?

PAUL. I'm good.

MARTIN. Of course, you are, Paul, of course, you are. Give me minute.

PAUL. Sure thing, Mr. Marcus. *(Martin exits. Paul goes back to his sandwich and script. Ethel Reed [Lois] enters. She is smoking.)*

ETHEL. Don't get up. *(Paul sees her and rises.)*

PAUL. Hi, I'm Paul Benjamin. I'll be playing Henry.

ETHEL. Is there only one chair?

PAUL. I'm sure they're bringing more.

ETHEL. An optimist.

PAUL. I saw some in the hall. I could …

ETHEL. Would you be a dear?

PAUL. No problem, take a load off. What's your name?

ETHEL. Pardon me?

PAUL. I'm Paul Benjamin.

ETHEL. Yes. *(She looks at him.)*

PAUL. I'll go get that chair. *(Ethel sits and Paul exits. Martin enters.)*

MARTIN. Ethel, you look amazing.

ETHEL. Are there no ash trays in this building?

MARTIN. I'll have the girl bring one in.

ETHEL. Don't bother; I'll use my hand.

MARTIN. Don't be surly.

ETHEL. Am I that ancient?

MARTIN. As what? As me?

ETHEL. As a young man in the theatrical profession doesn't recognize me.

MARTIN. He'd recognize your voice.

ETHEL. I spoke. Several sentences. *(Paul returns with a chair.)*

MARTIN. Paul, you must know Miss Ethel Reed from the La Tropicale Cigar Smokers Lounge.

ETHEL. Among other credits.

PAUL. What a hoot. My dad loved that show.

ETHEL. When are the others arriving? I hear this Elizabeth Hunter is a modern day marvel, but I was somewhat surprised, Martin, to hear that she'd be working in this production.

PAUL. I did *Seven Messengers* with Liz Hunter in try-outs. I was one of the messengers.

ETHEL. My script ends on page thirty; I assume there's more.

MARTIN. Ethel, you know I adore you.

ETHEL. An ash tray; is *that* too demanding?

MARTIN. I'll be right back. *(Martin exits.)*

PAUL. I worked with Jerry Ritt's brother once in a radio drama. *(Lulu enters with an ash tray which she holds out to Ethel.)*

ETHEL. Ah, you've saved me.

LULU. Miss Reed, it is an honor to meet you.

ETHEL. What a dear. Would you bring me some coffee? Mitzie knows how I like it. Tell her extra sweet.

LULU. Coming right up. *(Shaking Paul's hand.)* You must be Henry.

PAUL. I am. Paul Benjamin.

LULU. Lulu Miles. *(Tad enters.)* And may I present Tad Rose?

TAD. *(Shaking hands.)* Pleasure.

PAUL. Paul Benjamin. *(Martin enters.)*

MARTIN. Miss Miles, we need …

LULU. Six chairs.

TAD. Jerry's not coming?

MARTIN. They held him on the Coast. *(Lulu turns to go.)*

ETHEL. And my coffee, dear. Extra sweet.

LULU. Yes, Miss Reed.

MARTIN. *(Taking Lulu aside.)* There's a flask in my top drawer.

LULU. Excuse me?

MARTIN. "Extra sweet."

LULU. Oh. Right. *(Lulu exits.)*

ETHEL. Well, Mr. Rose, do we have pages?

TAD. Not quite to the end, but almost.

ETHEL. Almost: such an innocuous word. *(Tad begins distributing scripts. Lulu enters with two more chairs.)*

PAUL. I can't wait to see how it all turns out. Do you need help?

LULU. Sit; you're the talent. *(She exits.)*

TAD. We're only waiting on Miss Hunter?

MARTIN. Can I speak to you for a moment? *(Tad and Martin retreat to a corner.)*

PAUL. Nuts and bolts.

ETHEL. Excuse me?

PAUL. Production talk.

ETHEL. Quite. *(Lulu returns with two more chairs, bringing the total to six. She is setting them in a circle as an overly sexy young woman whom we haven't seen before enters. She is Suzie Tyrone.)*

LULU. Can I help you?

SUZIE. Is this Studio Six? I'm in Studio Six.

LULU. Yes, you are. What are you looking for?

SUZIE. Ummm, hold on ... *(Digging into her purse.)* I think my agent said Six.

LULU. This is Studio Six.

SUZIE. *(Still digging.)* For rehearsal. I think it was Six.

LULU. This is Six.

SUZIE. *(Holding up a piece of paper.)* Six!

LULU. We're having a rehearsal in here.

SUZIE. In Six. I'm Ruby.

LULU. Excuse me? *(Martin sees Suzie.)*

MARTIN. Suzie, is it possible you've grown even more stunning?

SUZIE. Marty.

MARTIN. Ethel Reed, Paul Benjamin — Suzie Tyrone. Lulu Miles, assisting us. And have you met our writer Tad Rose?

TAD. I saw you in *Bismark*. You were fascinating.

ETHEL. That's why you look familiar. Didn't you drown in that one?

MARTIN. Okay, as soon as we get those chairs ... great. Today we're going to give Tad a chance to hear what we've got. We'll have a completed script by Thursday.

TAD. Knock wood.

MARTIN. We'll have a completed script by Thursday. By then the night crew will have these set pieces in place. Everybody knows Jerry can't be here until day after tomorrow.

LULU. What is going on?

MARTIN. He got held up on the Coast.

LULU. What does she mean she's Ruby?

MARTIN. Yes, we're lucky to have Suzie signed on for the project.

LULU. We agreed on Elizabeth Hunter.

SUZIE. Oh.

MARTIN. Miss Miles, will you take your seat? We can discuss any confusion later.

LULU. Tad.

TAD. What?

LULU. Aren't you going to say something?

TAD. About what?

ETHEL. Liz Hunter's on the list, honey.

LULU. Elizabeth Hunter?

ETHEL. Is blacklisted.

MARTIN. Elizabeth Hunter was no longer right for the part.

LULU. There must be a mistake.

ETHEL. She was at that peace conference at the Waldorf three years ago, and that's all it takes.

LULU. When she was a teenager? And it was a peace conference.

PAUL. Elizabeth Hunter's a commie?

LULU. This is ridiculous. *(To Martin.)* You've got to do something. No offense to Miss Tyrone here who I'm sure is a terrific performer …

SUZIE. I got very wet on *Bismark* and never complained.

LULU. No one will be getting wet in this story.

SUZIE. My agent said in the flood scene.

LULU. It's a fire.

TAD. We'll see.

LULU. We'll what?

TAD. Budget nixed the fire.

LULU. You promised.

TAD. I didn't promise. We had to make some edits.

LULU. Edits?

MARTIN. The boys upstairs came down hard on the idea that this hick girl would have the technology before RCA.

LULU. But she did. I mean, that's the story that we agreed to.

TAD. She had a prototype, right? And she'll still have that. It just won't work as well as she'd have hoped.

LULU. But her prototype would've worked if it hadn't been destroyed.

TAD. Would've, could've, should've.

LULU. No, would've.

TAD. Don't be difficult.

LULU. Oh, I'm sorry, am I inappropriately standing up for what's right?

TAD. Lose the high horse. This is the real world.

LULU. As opposed to the coffee shop; your office; your bedroom. *(Ethel begins to cough loudly.)*

MARTIN. Let's suspend budget conversations for now.

LULU. What else has been changed?

TAD. Nothing important.

LULU. Just another "comrade" or two?

PAUL. Comrade?

TAD. You went along with that.

LULU. This is more than a word switch. It's the essence of the story. If you don't let Ruby invent the machine, you're rubbing out her life all over again. And if you don't let Liz Hunter play the part … You can't give in to this red-baiting hysteria. Mr. Marcus, if you don't hire that girl, no one will.

MARTIN. Maybe you haven't heard, Miss Miles, but I have hired a girl.

LULU. Don't let them do this.

MARTIN. Do what?

LULU. Turn you into a coward.

TAD. It's not cowardice.

PAUL. It's patriotism.

LULU. It's not illegal to go to a political conference. It's not illegal to be a communist for crying out loud.

SUZIE. Oh, I think it is.

LULU. This is America.

SUZIE. But not for communists.

PAUL. Don't kid yourself, miss, these people want to infiltrate our way of life.

LULU. Can you even define "infiltrate"?

PAUL. All I know is they're trying to infiltrate the Actors Studio.

LULU. Then they really must be a bunch of morons.

TAD. This isn't a joke.

LULU. Isn't it?

PAUL. There is a war going on.

LULU. I know that, but terrorizing some poor actress isn't going to bring those boys home.

MARTIN. We're being asked as Americans to state which side of the fence we're on. If you're not willing to declare your allegiance … then you're bringing this country down.

LULU. Martin, a person is allowed to look at this world and then dream of ways for it to be different. That's Ruby. An uncompromising vision of a changed world. Sabotaged. But it's us sabotaging now.

TAD. That's not what we're doing.

MARTIN. I am doing you a favor here, Miss Miles, by telling you to sit down and be quiet.

LULU. Why didn't I see this coming? You just can't let her succeed, can you?

MARTIN. Are you going to force me to throw you out of this studio?

LULU. No one's forcing you to do anything. You're choosing to accept this madness.

TAD. Lulu, please.

LULU. Please what? Please get on board with a bunch of shitheels making a mockery of everything true? No. No, I won't. Ruby is my story. I want it back.

TAD. Don't do this.

LULU. I won't let you destroy her all over again with condescending endings and some ditzy, soaking dancer.

SUZIE. I am not a dancer. *(Lulu starts grabbing scripts out of people's hands.)*

TAD. Lu, you're acting crazy.

MARTIN. Am I going to have to call Security?

LULU. Sure, call those goddamn FBI dropouts who run the upstairs office.

TAD. For god's sake, shut up.

LULU. It's my story. You know that.

TAD. No; *The Ruby Sunrise* is mine.

LULU. But it's not.

TAD. I wrote it; look at the goddamn cover page. *(Pause.)*

LULU. When did this become okay? It's like it's not even shameful anymore.

MARTIN. Lulu, this is your last warning.

LULU. Yeah. *(Lulu looks at Martin. She throws the scripts on the floor in disgust.)*

MARTIN. You're fired. *(Lulu exits. Tad makes a small move to follow her.)* Tad, sit down. *(Tad sits. Martin pulls the extra chair out of the circle. Paul collects the scripts from the floor.)* I apologize for the hectic-ness.

PAUL. No problem, Mr. Marcus.

SUZIE. We're all professionals.

MARTIN. Tad?

TAD. We're all professionals.

ETHEL. Where is that coffee?

MARTIN. Coming. Now, are there any logistics I'm forgetting? Paul, I know all this TV talk is new to you — it's pretty damn new to all of us — but you'll catch on quick.

PAUL. I'm catching on already.

MARTIN. Let's turn to page one. *(They all sit. The scripts are redistributed.)* Go ahead, Suzie. *(The read begins.)*

SUZIE. It happened just like this. I was on the mower, doing a boy's job on account of the war, plowing the earth in those straight, straight lines. My thoughts, as usual, weren't on farming; I was building something else in my mind.

Scene 6

On Set. Suzie and Paul have new script pages in hand. They are rehearsing in the bedroom area, not yet in costume. Martin and Tad watch.

SUZIE. *(As Ruby.)* What am I doing here?
PAUL. *(As Henry.)* You had an electrical shock. It threw you halfway across the barn. Don't you remember?
SUZIE. I've been sleeping?
PAUL. A bit.
SUZIE. But what happened?
PAUL. Something must have shorted.
SUZIE. What were we talking about? My father is coming.
PAUL. Don't worry about that now.
SUZIE. My Television is waiting.
PAUL. Whoa, lie back, lie back now. You need to rest.
SUZIE. Oh my goodness. Did the surge … *(Turning out to Tad.)* Surge?
TAD. Yes, surge.
MARTIN. Let's keep going.
SUZIE. Did the surge fry the connections?
PAUL. You know I wouldn't know about that.
SUZIE. I have to get back to work.
PAUL. Rest now. It's not as if that contraption's gonna burst into flames the moment you close your eyes.
SUZIE. Flames. Why do you say flames? Henry, what's become of my Television?
PAUL. I'll check on it, okay, I'll check on it.
SUZIE. Unhook the blue leads from the generator. They're tied with blue string; that's how you'll recognize them.
PAUL. What would happen if I connected the yellow leads instead of the blue?
SUZIE. Don't ever do that! If the generator's still running, especially if the more dangerous chemicals were knocked over, the whole thing would blow to Kingdom Come.
TAD. Stop, just stop.

MARTIN. Tad.

SUZIE. What's wrong?

TAD. It's not you; it's me. It's the dialogue.

SUZIE. I think it's great, the dialogue. *(Ethel enters in Lois costume.)*

ETHEL. Are you on break? Wonderful. I need something addressed: "May you never feel what it feels: to want something more than anything in the world, and not only is it ripped from you but, also, it's exposed as poison."

TAD. What about it?

ETHEL. Clunk clunk clunk.

MARTIN. We're not quite ready for you, Ethel.

ETHEL. I was told light check at two. And I saw the technical supervisor in the hall.

MARTIN. Shit. Who's got blocking notes?

TAD. Audio stuck his head in about ten minutes ago.

MARTIN. I'm talking about the goddamn blocking notes.

SUZIE. Marty?

MARTIN. *(Too loud.)* What!

SUZIE. Are you mad at me?

MARTIN. No. No, Suzie. Suzie, go down to Costume. Paul, will you escort Suzie down to Costume?

PAUL. Sure thing, Mr. Marcus.

MARTIN. Tad, get over here. *(Suzie and Paul exit.)*

TAD. I'm not changing the Lois speech.

MARTIN. Fuck the speech; Ethel can make anything sing. When did we go back to a fire?

TAD. Flood's not working.

MARTIN. Budget's going to lynch me, and that means you.

TAD. It doesn't flood in Indianapolis in May.

MARTIN. It doesn't ... what the fuck are you talking about? Are we making a teleplay here or pissing off the Empire State Building? *(Ethel is seated on set, applying age make-up.)*

ETHEL. "All your dreams were built on a basket of lies." Is it me, or is that a mixed metaphor?

MARTIN. This is just to test the lights, Ethel.

TAD. Martin, I need Lulu. I need her back on set.

MARTIN. I miss the girl, too. But it's spilled milk: We cry over it after we broadcast.

TAD. If we broadcast.

MARTIN. We are going to broadcast. You will not leave me in the lurch here.

TAD. Are you threatening me now? Going to get me listed in Red Channels?

MARTIN. You want to pretend your hands are clean because you never had to fire anybody, be my guest, but do it on your own time. Now wipe your ass and get me an ending that works. *(Suzie enters in costume: a slinky night gown.)*

SUZIE. *(To Ethel.)* Oh, Ethel, you look so old! Do you think this is too see-through? Paul said it was fine. *(Tad exits.)*

MARTIN. Why don't you get set, Suzie? You look great. *(Suzie lies down.)*

MARTIN. Who's in the booth? We don't need music. Clear the fucking musicians, and get the contrast man in there.

SUZIE. Good night, Marty.

MARTIN. Good night, dear. *(Calling out.)* We're ready. Let's do it. *(Suzie closes her eyes. Ethel stows her make-up kit away. She positions herself close to "sleeping" Suzie. The lights close in as if it is late at night. Ethel takes a wash cloth and dabs Suzie's forehead gently.)*

ETHEL. *(As Lois.)* Oh, Ruby. I let you down. I wanted for you what I wanted for myself a long time ago. I thought you could mold your dreams into a more viable form, and that it would spare you the kind of pain that I felt, that I still feel, everyday.

MARTIN. Hold. Hold. "Viable"?

ETHEL. Yes.

MARTIN. What viable?

ETHEL. Viable. It means …

MARTIN. I don't give a damn what it means. Ethel, where are you getting this dialogue? For scene ten, I have …

ETHEL. I am aware of what is scrawled on the cue cards, Martin, but *instinct.* I have a very strong instinct that issues of viability cut to the heart of this play.

MARTIN. That's interesting, Ethel, because I, too, have a very strong instinct right about now.

SUZIE. *(Opening her eyes.)* I have an instinct, too.

MARTIN. Do you now?

SUZIE. I think Ruby should have really bad teeth. Like on a farm.

MARTIN. Are the musicians still there? *(Calling out.)* I think it's as good a time as any to test the score. Music. I said, music! *(And the music comes.)*

Scene 7

The set in the TV studio is starting to come together. On one side, the Kitchen; on the other, the Barn with all the TV equipment in it. A simply dressed young woman (Elizabeth Hunter) enters and looks around at the stage. Tad enters. He seems shocked by the sight of her. He watches her. Finally she notices him.

ELIZABETH. I'm sorry; I was only looking around; I'm just leaving.

TAD. No, it's okay. *(Tad stares at her.)*

ELIZABETH. Are you Security?

TAD. No.

ELIZABETH. Do I know you?

TAD. No. I don't think so. I mean I recognize you. You're an actress.

ELIZABETH. Guilty as charged. Are you involved in this production?

TAD. No. Are you?

ELIZABETH. No. No.

TAD. What are you doing here then?

ELIZABETH. You're sure you're not Security?

TAD. I'm the opposite. I'm insecurity.

ELIZABETH. Do you know Martin Marcus?

TAD. The producer?

ELIZABETH. He tried to get me some extra work on the variety they're shooting upstairs.

TAD. He did that?

ELIZABETH. It didn't work out so well.

TAD. Why not?

ELIZABETH. Good luck getting an answer on that one. No one will even admit to me that there is a list, anywhere, no less that I'm on it, but somehow I find myself in a permanent state of "no longer right for the part." Today, I was literally going to be a pair of legs in a crowd scene. You wouldn't even see my profile. But some advertising agency guy spotted me: Is that Liz Hunter? Get her out of here.

I said, no, I'm nobody, just a brunette trying earn a nickel. Get her out of here.

TAD. They're maniacs.

ELIZABETH. I think "maniac" is generous: It excuses their collaboration.

TAD. Can I have your autograph?

ELIZABETH. My autograph?

TAD. I saw you in *Saint Joan* at the Lyceum. You're tremendous.

ELIZABETH. I don't think the autograph will be worth much.

TAD. Don't say that; you're a rising star.

ELIZABETH. But it's true: my career is officially over. I guess I learned that today.

TAD. You were slated to perform on this set?

ELIZABETH. Slated? I don't know. I read the first act.

TAD. What was it about?

ELIZABETH. Despair. I mean, persistence.

TAD. Huh.

ELIZABETH. It happened just like this. I was on the mower, doing a boy's job on account of the war, plowing the earth in those straight, straight lines. My thoughts, as usual, weren't on farming; I was building something else in my mind. I didn't even notice that the reins had slipped from my hands until the horse lurched forward. And right as I felt that jerk, right then, that was my Eureka. You gotta magnetically deflect electrons across a Television screen in the same way you plow a field. Back and forth, line by line, row by row by row. I had a vision in a potato field. Almost wish I hadn't 'cause I knew how hard it was gonna be, and it was gonna be hard. But I saw my destiny: to romance the electron. Been following that path ever since.

TAD. You learned the opening speech?

ELIZABETH. I know the first act by heart.

TAD. You must have an amazing memory.

ELIZABETH. It's a curse. *(Beat.)* You're familiar with the play?

TAD. A little. The first act.

ELIZABETH. You still want that signature?

TAD. *(Searching.)* I don't have any paper.

ELIZABETH. A writer without paper.

TAD. How'd you know I'm a writer?

ELIZABETH. A certain smell. Overworked and underappreciated. *(Going in her bag.)* I've got a publicity photo in here somewhere — might as well use them up — how would that suit you?

TAD. That would be amazing.

ELIZABETH. Who should I make it out to?

TAD. Mitch.

ELIZABETH. Just Mitch?

TAD. Mitch is good. *(She writes on the picture.)* I don't believe your career is over. You're too talented; it can't be right.

ELIZABETH. I didn't say it was right; I said it was over. *(She holds the picture out to him. He hesitates.)* What's wrong?

TAD. My name is Tad Rose, and I'm sorry.

ELIZABETH. You didn't seem like a Mitch.

TAD. I'm sorry.

ELIZABETH. You said that already.

TAD. I can't get you back on the show. I'm just a writer, a lowly writer, and not even a very successful one.

ELIZABETH. Don't you want to read what I wrote?

TAD. What?

ELIZABETH. My autograph. *(He takes the picture and reads.)*

TAD. Dear Mr. Rose, May God Forgive Us All.

ELIZABETH. I had such dreams. New York City. I was going to be the best they'd ever seen.

TAD. You could testify, you know. They'd welcome you back. You were young and made a big mistake. Sign right here.

ELIZABETH. Would you do that?

TAD. I don't know what I would do.

ELIZABETH. But you do know. You wrote this play. About what it means to follow your vision, no matter the cost.

TAD. Yeah, it means you feel miserable when you fail to accomplish what you set out to do, and in the end, no one's ever heard of you.

ELIZABETH. Is that what happens to Ruby: She fails?

TAD. Oh no: She wins. She gets to marry Henry.

ELIZABETH. So all her work, that doesn't count for anything in your world?

TAD. It's not my world. It's *the* world: the way it is.

ELIZABETH. And Ruby's mistake was thinking she could change things. Crazy. *(Beat.)* Mr. Rose, would you give me my picture back please?

TAD. Your picture?

ELIZABETH. I thought you believed in this girl. I thought you named her sunrise for a reason. You don't believe in anything. I don't think God should forgive that. *(He hands the picture back to her.)*

TAD. Do you want me to leave you alone here? I'll make sure no one comes in.

ELIZABETH. No. No, I'm done. *(Beat.)* I'm done. *(She exits, leaving him alone.)*

Scene 8

Lulu in the coffee shop, eating soup. Ethel enters.

ETHEL. How's the soup?

LULU. Watery. *(Looking up.)* Miss Reed. What are you doing in a place like this?

ETHEL. Is that a pick-up line?

LULU. No ...

ETHEL. You're throwing a pass at me?

LULU. I'm surprised to see you here. This dump is hardly of your caliber. *(Ethel sits.)*

ETHEL. You think I'm a snob.

LULU. No.

ETHEL. I think you're a snob.

LULU. I'm not a snob.

ETHEL. We are selling a detergent; you are aware of that? That is the purpose of our jobs in this emerging field.

LULU. I don't have a job. I was fired.

ETHEL. You can't be too literal in this business. Fire can mean many things.

LULU. It's not a fire; it's a flood. Haven't you heard?

ETHEL. Actually, they've reduced it to a severe thunderstorm. And it might be scattered clouds before the day is out, but that in no way excuses what you did.

LULU. What I did? I was the only one being rational.

ETHEL. Screaming in a rehearsal hall?

LULU. But I was right!

ETHEL. You called your employer a shitheel.

LULU. I'm unclear about what it is you want, Miss Reed.

ETHEL. I want the rush of emotion. When I'm sitting in my dressing room, memorizing the new pages in my hand as the make-up boy sets my curls.

LULU. That gives you a rush?

ETHEL. It can. You know it can. The calm before the storm when everyone on set hums with a silent electricity, doing our jobs to perfection, or the best human approximation we can muster; and who knows what the next hour will bring, but we're as ready as one can ever be. And then when I go out under the lights, when I know I have one chance, to get it beautifully and do it effortlessly, live on camera, right now. One shot at nailing it because when this moment passes, it's gone. Everyone from my sister-in-law to the milkman will either get it or not. And praying that the camera focus holds, and no sound bleeds in from the radio Western they're broadcasting down the hall, and here it comes: They're shooting. I know precisely what I have to do for all you lovely, sad people at home, and I do, and it goes out on the airwaves, and it's done when Jerry Ritt calls wrap. I want to sell some detergent.

LULU. I wanted that, too. From my first day of work at the local station in Indiana. More live than live, I never felt so alive. And god, the stories I wanted to tell.

ETHEL. Yet off you go throwing tantrums. Not that it wasn't impressive — hell, I've never seen anything like it in my life and I'll remember it until that day I die — but, young lady, you have to know your place. Even Ethel Reed has to know her place.

LULU. Oh, for heaven's sake: Ethel Reed does exactly what she wants.

ETHEL. No, I do exactly what they want. For me, all this … *(Gesturing vaguely to herself.)* … grows a little tiresome.

LULU. You don't look tired.

ETHEL. I'll loan you my make-up. Even a script girl needs make-up when she's going back to work in the morning.

LULU. How can I go back to work?

ETHEL. The subway is running, dear, if you can't afford a cab.

LULU. Go back to a place where any day of the week, some moron can corner you and ask you to start naming names?

ETHEL. I don't recall anyone asking you to name anything.

LULU. But isn't that just luck?

ETHEL. Then it's good luck. Because you can walk back through that door and make things better.

LULU. Better?

ETHEL. "What's so bad about better?"

LULU. Why do you care?

ETHEL. Because the second act is schlock. Have you read the drivel they want me to say?

LULU. No. Why do you care?

ETHEL. Because I am an old bag who works in the theater; and we can't afford any more losses. *(Ethel rises.)* Your soup is getting cold.

LULU. It was cold when it arrived.

ETHEL. My advice is: Eat it anyway.

Scene 9

On Set: the Barn and the Kitchen from Lois' house in Indiana. Tad sits alone at the kitchen table. There is a liquor bottle in front of him. He drinks. Lulu enters. He doesn't see her. She hesitates. Finally …

LULU. You look awful. *(Tad looks up.)*

TAD. I haven't been sleeping so good.

LULU. I know what that's like.

TAD. I telephoned you. I telephoned twenty times.

LULU. It rang and rang in the hall.

TAD. Why didn't you answer? *(Lulu walks over to the barn area of the set.)*

LULU. I didn't know what to say then.

TAD. You know now?

LULU. Yeah, I do. *(Lulu hits the prop TV equipment with her fist.)*

TAD. Hey. *(She bangs it again.)*

LULU. I'm nothing. I'm nobody.

TAD. Cut it out. *(Lulu pushes the prop over. It falls to the floor.)*

LULU. I've failed. I'm nothing.

TAD. Lu. *(She bangs on the equipment. Tad tries to restrain her.)*

LULU. It's done for, dead. It's over.

TAD. You want Security to come in here?

LULU. *(Struggling against him.)* You betrayed me. You horrible chicken. You didn't stand up for me.

TAD. I didn't know how.

LULU. You built something with me. You had a stake in it. Our photo-cathode tube. *(Breaking away from him.)* Now, my career is fin-

ished. *(Lulu continues banging and overturning props in the barn set.)*
TAD. Stop it.
LULU. No one's ever heard of me.
TAD. No.
LULU. I've been erased. *(Lulu grabs the liquor bottle which Tad was drinking from and smashes it against the wall. It shatters.)*
TAD. What the hell are you doing?
LULU. Working on a scene.
TAD. A scene?
LULU. A scene I never told you about, but it's the truth. Ruby destroyed the lab herself. The only flames in that barn were the ones she set.
TAD. No.
LULU. Yes. By the time she recovered from the electrical shock, there was news about Farnsworth and Zworykin in the papers. She knew she could never catch up to those guys — it was over for her — so she shattered it all and ran away. Nothing to show for her labor; except, of course, a little girl who never seemed quite able to please her.
TAD. Oh, Lulu …
LULU. Don't. I talked to Mr. Marcus. I apologized for calling him a shitheel. He said it was his favorite swear word and offered to re-hire me.
TAD. You're back?
LULU. I'm here to help you finish your teleplay. *(Lulu begins to clean up the prop equipment that she knocked about.)*
TAD. Leave that stuff alone.
LULU. I've got to clean up my mess. There's going to be a rehears-al in an hour's time.
TAD. But it's broken.
LULU. It's a prop, Tad; it doesn't have to work.
TAD. We'll get someone else to clean it up.
LULU. I can do it.
TAD. No, I can do it. You have to get to work.
LULU. I am working. I'm doing my job.
TAD. Then it's the wrong job. Your job is to tell those stories you're always going off about. How it's all going to be democratic, and the little guy's going to have his day, and sure, he might not get it right off, and sometimes he'll drink too much, but he's trying, and he's a person — a struggling, tired, breathing, beautiful person — and we shouldn't just throw him in the garbage.

LULU. Maybe I *was* crazy, spouting all that stuff. It's almost embarrassing.

TAD. What's embarrassing: that you thought it shouldn't be easy to throw people away?

LULU. But it is easy with some people.

TAD. Then you've got to invent a new ending for them, Lu. Pull your mom out of the trash.

LULU. I tried. I failed.

TAD. But you didn't give up. You persisted. Can't that be your story?

LULU. Don't you get it: I don't know what the story is anymore. Mine or hers. All I can see is a gutted barn with the life torn out of it; a gutted life.

TAD. Because you're lost. That's all. It happens sometimes. You feel lost right now. And it's my fault. I took something from you, in front of all those people. And God might not forgive me, but I've got to give it back. Sit down.

LULU. What? *(Tad gets a typewriter. He puts a piece of paper in it.)*

TAD. Please sit down.

LULU. You want me to type?

TAD. Yes. A new title page. With your name added on. You want some coffee?

LULU. I should bring you coffee; you're the writer.

TAD. Not once you get your name on the title page, I'm not. I'm the co-writer.

LULU. Co-writer.

TAD. Five seconds in the credits. I know it's not much, but once we get a stronger union, we'll fight for more. And we'll fight to sneak in a thing or two or three, things that matter to us, into our scripts, under the radar, along with all compromises. And we'll just keep knocking on that glass screen in people's living rooms until they sober up and tune in.

LULU. What happened to you?

TAD. You. Liz. Ruby. All you goddamn crazy girls from Kokomo. *(Pause. She looks at the typewriter.)*

LULU. Sneaking into people's living rooms: You make it sound like we're criminals.

TAD. Can I ask you something?

LULU. Is it personal?

TAD. Very.

LULU. You can ask; I might not answer.

TAD. How did Ruby get the nickname "Sunrise"?

LULU. That's what you want to ask me?

TAD. That's where I want to start. *(Lulu crosses to the type-writer. She sits.)*

LULU. Milk, three sugars.

TAD. Coming right up.

LULU. And when you get back, we can start arguing about what a ruby sunrise means.

End of Part Two

PART THREE

*The following scene is played on the Studio Set and simultane-
ously shown live on a Television Screen (or screens). All the per-
formances are first-rate. A countdown to the TV shoot is heard.*

COUNTDOWN. Ten seconds! *(And then.)* Five, four, three, two ...
*(A silent beat for "one," and the shoot begins ... The sound of rain falling
hard. Ethel dressed as Lois sits at the kitchen table. A red glass bottle of
booze before her. Paul enters, dressed in costume as Henry. He is wet.)*
PAUL. Where is she? Where the heck is she? My wallet's gone.
(Ethel doesn't respond.) Do you know where she is, Miss Haver? I
think she stole my wallet.
ETHEL. She didn't steal your wallet.
PAUL. Fine, borrowed. Did she teach you to say that?
ETHEL. *I* stole your wallet.
PAUL. What?
ETHEL. She had to get out of here before her daddy shows. I
handed over your cash and sent her to the train.
PAUL. I should've believed in her more. For real, believed.
ETHEL. Henry, no way in hell a Television was gonna spring
forth from that barn. Too much working against it. It just wasn't
viable. *(Suzie [as Ruby] enters the scene. She is very wet. She carries a
suitcase.)* What are you still doing here?
PAUL. Miss Haver said you'd left already.
SUZIE. I did, but I couldn't, not like that. I took your money
'cause I wanted to punish you. I was so mad about what you said
that night in the barn.
PAUL. I'm sorry about what I said. And I'm so sorry about what
happened to your lab.
SUZIE. Who would've thought it? At this time of year: a flood?
PAUL. We can put all that behind us now, Ruby Sunrise.
SUZIE. You don't even know what that name means.
PAUL. I do.
SUZIE. If you knew what it meant, you wouldn't think saying that
would keep me here. Oh, Henry. Tell him, Aunt Lois.

ETHEL. It's a story about a little girl who's sad and bruised, 'cause her world's sad and bruised. She takes a red liquor bottle from the table and holds it up to the window, up to the light. "It's called a lens," she says. "It changes the way you see things, so the whole world's made of redness." She says, "I'm gonna change the world, Aunt Lois."

SUZIE. "I'm gonna make everything a sunrise." I have to, Henry. *(Suzie digs into her pocket, and takes out a couple of crumpled bills. She holds them out to Henry.)*

PAUL. What are you doing? I don't want that.

SUZIE. You gave me a lot. I'm not going to take your money.

PAUL. Where do you think you're gonna go? You got no place to go.

SUZIE. I don't know. San Francisco? Philo Farnsworth's found a way to produce a carrier wave which cuts down on interference from the synchronizing currents; and he's trying to patent a process to get rid of the ghost image caused by the return scan line. I got some ideas about that myself. Maybe, I'll try New Jersey: Edison Labs. Or New York City. You think RCA could find a job for a farm girl from Indiana?

PAUL. Big corporation like that, they'll own everything you invent.

ETHEL. She's doing what she has to do.

PAUL. By destroying the most precious part of herself?

SUZIE. No. This is me trying *not* to destroy. Because if I don't do this, I'll shatter it all in a rage, I swear, every last piece of everything 'til there's nothing left. I know it's sad. But I feel like this is the only way it won't be sad forever. Take your money, Henry.

PAUL. Keep it.

SUZIE. You're giving it to me?

PAUL. You stay here, you got nothing; I get that. You go out there, maybe you can change the way people see things, like you said.

SUZIE. I might not get it right off.

PAUL. You gotta start where you start. If I had a daughter, I guess I'd tell her to do what you're doing.

SUZIE. You'll have a daughter one day, Henry. She'll be so pretty, and so kind. And her mother will be so lucky.

PAUL. I think you better go now.

SUZIE. Henry.

PAUL. Yeah?

SUZIE. Do I scare you?

PAUL. Yeah. But why do you ask?

SUZIE. Because you still haven't tried to kiss me. *(And they kiss.)*

ETHEL. *(Clearing her throat.)* A-hem. *(The kids stop kissing. Ethel approaches and hands Suzie the bottle of booze.)* Hide this good. And use it when you're making all your special vacuums.

SUZIE. There's gonna be an all-electrical system sending pictures through the air before the year is out. You believe me now?

ETHEL. Not if you miss that train, there's not.

SUZIE. Not gonna. No way I'm gonna miss. *(Suzie exits with her suitcase and the bottle of alcohol. The rain beats down.)*

PAUL. You got a drink, Miss Haver?

ETHEL. No, Henry, I do not. Packed the last away with your girl-friend.

PAUL. You think she's my girlfriend?

ETHEL. As much as she could ever be anybody's.

PAUL. So it's some kind of upbeat ending after all.

ETHEL. Some kind.

PAUL. *(Seeing out the window.)* Hey, someone's coming up the road.

ETHEL. Oh hell.

PAUL. It's her daddy, come to stop her?

ETHEL. Must be.

PAUL. But Ruby's on her way now. She's already on her way. *(Ethel rises. She crosses to the edge of the set and looks out a window.)*

ETHEL. I'll be.

PAUL. What?

ETHEL. What a hopeless woman I am.

PAUL. What are you talking about?

ETHEL. That man, he still looks good to me. After all he's done. Hopeless.

PAUL. Maybe he's changed. Maybe you can change him.

ETHEL. Here comes heartache.

PAUL. Make him better.

ETHEL. Here comes pain. *(The camera fades away from Ethel and Henry and comes up on Suzie on a different part of the set. She is walking in place in front of a back-drop of the house which slowly recedes, making it appear on the TV screen(s) that she is walking away from the house. She has an determined step.)*

SUZIE. *(V.O.)* Television's gonna change people. I know it can. It'll be a whole different world once people can see the world right in their own homes. *(Lulu approaches a Television screen. She watches "Ruby's" departure on the little box.)* You'll get to watch the news as it's happening; can you imagine? Or listen to somebody talk while you're looking at them, too; somebody far far away that you'd never get to meet, and maybe that person has something to teach you. A

62

lecture about science or safety, or a story. *(Tad, Martin, Ethel, and Paul gather to watch this final image on a monitor.)* We'll get pictures from all over the world, and learn about our comrades in other countries, heck, other planets. We won't be able to hide from the truth anymore. We'll understand how things really are. And how they could be. That's how it could be. *(Ruby enters the space. She crosses to her daughter and the TV screen.)* Go on, call me crazy, the Crazy Girl from Kokomo, but I just know there'll come a time when all our differences will be settled around tables, instead of going to war. Television will be the end of war 'cause who could bear it? Who could bear to see war right in your own living room? *(The music swells over Suzie's speech. Ruby and Lulu watch together as "The End" flashes on the TV screen. The two women almost touch as the lights begin to fade ... And the credits on the TV screen begin to roll.)*

End of Play

PROPERTY LIST

Cleaning rags
Parts of disassembled generator
Can or bottle of kerosene
Lantern
Large piece of wood
Pair of wires
Coffee pot
Lamp or wall switch to turn on light
Red bottle of whiskey
Parts of disassembled radio
Table with ringstands, clamps, meshed metal screen, cathode,
    wires, forceps, glass tube
2 torches
Cold cloth
Piece of paper
Copy of *Variety* 1952
Cup of coffee
Bowl of soup
Telephone
Sandwich
Cigarette
Ashtray
TV scripts
4 chairs
Make-up kit
Celebrity photo
Pen
TV equipment
Typewriter
Television screen(s)
Crumpled dollar bills

SOUND EFFECTS

Quick double ring of phone
Heavy rain